TRAVEL

places to go...
sites to see...
things to do...

PETER PAUPER PRESS, INC.
WHITE PLAINS, NEW YORK

Cover illustration & design by Taryn R. Sefecka

Cover and interior visa stamps image
copyright © Media Bakery/Digital Vision

Copyright © 2006
Peter Pauper Press, Inc.
202 Mamaroneck Avenue
White Plains, NY 10601
All rights reserved
ISBN 978-1-59359-428-2
Printed in China
17

Visit us at www.peterpauper.com